1954

Fun Facts & Trivia

ISBN: 9798865445449

© Spotty Dog Publications 2023
All Rights Reserved

INDEX

	Page
Calendar	4
People in High Office	5
British News & Events	9
Worldwide News & Events	18
Births - U.K. Personalities	31
Notable British Deaths	36
Popular Music	39
Top 5 Films	43
Sporting Winners	54
Cost of Living	62

FIRST EDITION

1954

January
M	T	W	T	F	S	S
				1	2	3
4	5	6	7	8	9	10
11	12	13	14	15	16	17
18	19	20	21	22	23	24
25	26	27	28	29	30	31

●:5 ◐:12 ○:19 ◑:27

February
M	T	W	T	F	S	S
1	2	3	4	5	6	7
8	9	10	11	12	13	14
15	16	17	18	19	20	21
22	23	24	25	26	27	28

●:3 ◐:10 ○:17 ◑:25

March
M	T	W	T	F	S	S
1	2	3	4	5	6	7
8	9	10	11	12	13	14
15	16	17	18	19	20	21
22	23	24	25	26	27	28
29	30	31				

●:5 ◐:11 ○:19 ◑:27

April
M	T	W	T	F	S	S
			1	2	3	4
5	6	7	8	9	10	11
12	13	14	15	16	17	18
19	20	21	22	23	24	25
26	27	28	29	30		

●:3 ◐:10 ○:18 ◑:26

May
M	T	W	T	F	S	S
					1	2
3	4	5	6	7	8	9
10	11	12	13	14	15	16
17	18	19	20	21	22	23
24	25	26	27	28	29	30
31						

●:2 ◐:9 ○:17 ◑:25

June
M	T	W	T	F	S	S
	1	2	3	4	5	6
7	8	9	10	11	12	13
14	15	16	17	18	19	20
21	22	23	24	25	26	27
28	29	30				

●:1 ◐:8 ○:16 ◑:23 ●:30

July
M	T	W	T	F	S	S
			1	2	3	4
5	6	7	8	9	10	11
12	13	14	15	16	17	18
19	20	21	22	23	24	25
26	27	28	29	30	31	

◐:8 ○:16 ◑:23 ●:29

August
M	T	W	T	F	S	S
						1
2	3	4	5	6	7	8
9	10	11	12	13	14	15
16	17	18	19	20	21	22
23	24	25	26	27	28	29
30	31					

◐:6 ○:14 ◑:21 ●:28

September
M	T	W	T	F	S	S
		1	2	3	4	5
6	7	8	9	10	11	12
13	14	15	16	17	18	19
20	21	22	23	24	25	26
27	28	29	30			

◐:5 ○:12 ◑:19 ●:27

October
M	T	W	T	F	S	S
				1	2	3
4	5	6	7	8	9	10
11	12	13	14	15	16	17
18	19	20	21	22	23	24
25	26	27	28	29	30	31

◐:5 ○:12 ◑:18 ●:26

November
M	T	W	T	F	S	S
1	2	3	4	5	6	7
8	9	10	11	12	13	14
15	16	17	18	19	20	21
22	23	24	25	26	27	28
29	30					

◐:3 ○:10 ◑:17 ●:25

December
M	T	W	T	F	S	S
		1	2	3	4	5
6	7	8	9	10	11	12
13	14	15	16	17	18	19
20	21	22	23	24	25	26
27	28	29	30	31		

◐:3 ○:10 ◑:17 ●:25

PEOPLE IN HIGH OFFICE

Monarch - Queen Elizabeth II
Reign: 6th February 1952 - 8th September 2022
Predecessor: King George VI
Successor: King Charles III

United Kingdom

Prime Minister
Winston Churchill
Conservative Party
26th October 1951 - 5th April 1955

Australia

Prime Minister
Sir Robert Menzies
Liberal (Coalition)
19th December 1949
- 26th January 1966

Canada

Prime Minister
Louis St. Laurent
Liberal Party
15th November 1948
- 21st June 1957

United States

President
Dwight D. Eisenhower
Republican Party
20th January 1953
- 20th January 1961

Brazil	President Getúlio Vargas (1951-1954) João Café Filho (1954-1955)
China	Premier Chen Cheng (1950-1954) Yu Hung-Chun (1954-1958)
Cuba	President Fulgencio Batista (1952-1959)
France	President Vincent Auriol (1947-1954) René Coty (1954-1959)
India	Prime Minister Jawaharlal Nehru (1947-1964)
Ireland	Taoiseach of Ireland Éamon de Valera (1951-1954) John A. Costello (1954-1957)
Italy	Prime Minister Giuseppe Pella (1953-1954) Amintore Fanfani (1954) Mario Scelba (1954-1955)
Japan	Prime Minister Shigeru Yoshida (1948-1954) Ichirō Hatoyama (1954-1956)

Mexico	President Adolfo Ruiz Cortines (1952-1958)
New Zealand	Prime Minister Sidney Holland (1949-1957)
Pakistan	Prime Minister Mohammad Ali Bogra (1953-1955)
Spain	President Francisco Franco (1938-1973)
South Africa	Prime Minister Daniel François Malan (1948-1954) Johannes Gerhardus Strijdom (1954-1958)
Soviet Union	Communist Party Leader Nikita Khrushchev (1953-1964)
Turkey	Prime Minister Adnan Menderes (1950-1960)
West Germany	Chancellor Konrad Adenauer (1949-1963)

BRITISH NEWS & EVENTS

JAN

10th | BOAC Flight 781, a British Overseas Airways Corporation de Havilland Comet jet airliner flying from Singapore to London, crashes in the Mediterranean Sea after suffering an explosive decompression at altitude; all 35 people on board are killed.

14th | Sandy Wilson's musical "The Boy Friend" opens at Wyndham's Theatre in London's West End. *NB: Immensely popular with the British public (including the Queen) it ran for more than five years - 2,082 performances.*

25th | The foreign ministers of the United States (John Foster Dulles), Britain (Anthony Eden), France (Georges Bidault), and the Soviet Union (Vyacheslav Molotov), meet at the Berlin Conference (25th January to 18th February 1954) but fail to reach an agreement on issues of European security and the international status of Germany and Austria.

25th | The BBC makes its first broadcast of Dylan Thomas's radio play "Under Milk Wood" on the Third Programme (two months after the author's death). *Notes: The play was recorded with a distinguished all-Welsh cast and included Richard Burton as "First Voice".*

FEB

10th January: Great Britain's team of Jean Westwood and Lawrence Demmy win the World Figure Skating Championship for the third consecutive time in Oslo, Norway. *Fun facts: Westwood and Demmy would go on to win again in 1955 and were inducted into the World Figure Skating Hall of Fame in 1977.*

FEB

12th | The Minister of Health, Iain MacLeod, and Medical Research Council (MRC) officials attend a press conference warning of the dangers of excessive smoking after a cohort study suggests the existence of a link between smoking and lung cancer.

MAR

22nd | Closed since 1939, the London gold bullion market reopens.

23rd March: The film Doctor in the House, based on the 1952 novel by Richard Gordon and starring Dirk Bogarde, is released. *Fun facts: Doctor in the House was the most popular box office film of 1954 in Great Britain. Its success spawned six sequels and a television and radio series. Photo (from left): Kenneth More, Kay Kendall and Dirk Bogarde in scene from Doctor in the House (1954).*

24th | After an eight-day trial at Winchester Assizes, The Lord Montagu of Beaulieu, his cousin Michael Pitt-Rivers, and their friend Peter Wildeblood are convicted of "conspiracy to incite certain male persons to commit serious offences with male persons". Lord Montagu is sentenced to twelve months in prison for "consensual homosexual offences"; Pitt-Rivers and Wildeblood are both sentenced to eighteen months.

30th | West Indian cricketer Garfield "Garry" Sobers makes his Test Cricket debut vs England at Sabina Park in Kingston, Jamaica. *Fun facts: Sobers is widely considered to be cricket's greatest ever all-rounder and one of the greatest cricketers of all time. He was knighted by Queen Elizabeth II in 1975 for his services to cricket.*

APR

3rd April: Oxford wins the 100th Boat Race. *Photo: Oxford (left) leading Cambridge as the Centenary University boat race passes Hammersmith Bridge in west London.*

9th	BBC Television broadcasts the opening episode of The Grove Family, the very first British TV soap opera. *NB: The series was broadcast live (as was common for British television at the time) and today just three of the original 148 episodes survive in the archives.*
14th	Aneurin Bevan resigns from the Labour Party's Shadow Cabinet over the Labour leadership's uncritical reaction to a statement, by Deputy Prime Minister Anthony Eden, regarding the Anglo-American decision to examine the possibility of a multi-national defence organisation in Asia and the Pacific.
24th	Wolverhampton Wanderers win the Football League First Division title for the first time in their history.
25th	Mau Mau Uprising: British troops carry out Operation Anvil, a military operation to remove suspected Mau Mau from Nairobi. The operation takes two weeks by which time some 20,000 Mau Mau suspects have been taken to Langata Camp, and some 30,000 more have been deported to the reserves. *NB: Operation Anvil would mark a turning-point in the British campaign against the Mau Mau.*

MAY

6th	Roger Bannister, with the help of pacemakers Chris Chataway and Chris Brasher, becomes the first person to break the four-minute mile with a time of 3m:59.4s. *Fun facts: As of June 2022, the "four-minute barrier" has been broken by 1,755 athletes. The current record is 3m:43.13s and was set by Hicham El Guerrouj of Morocco in July 1999.*

MAY

Photo: Athlete Roger Bannister crosses the line at Oxford University's Iffley Road Track to become the first person to ever run a sub-4-minute mile, 6th May 1954.

13th	The Labour Party makes sweeping gains from the Conservatives for the third successive year in the borough council elections. They gain some 505 seats and capture 11 local councils, losing just two to their opponents.
29th	Diane Leather becomes the first woman to break the five-minute mile with a time of 4m:59.6s during the Midlands Women's AAA Championships at Birmingham's Alexander Sports Ground. *Fun fact: The current women's record is 4m:07.64 and was set by Faith Kipyegon of Kenya in July 2023.*

JUN

7th	British cryptanalyst, mathematician and computer scientist Alan Turing, age 41, commits suicide by cyanide poisoning. *Notes: Turing is widely considered to be the father of theoretical computer science and his work was key to breaking the wartime Enigma codes.*
12th	An Irish Republican Army unit carries out a successful raid on Gough Barracks in Armagh, Northern Ireland, seizing 340 rifles, 50 sten guns, 12 bren guns, and a number of small arms. The raid gains international attention and signals a renewal in IRA activity following a long hiatus.
30th	From Greenwich to Glasgow thousands of skywatchers, using smoked glass or overexposed film, see at least 75% of the sun obscured during an eclipse of the sun.

JUL

2nd	England cricketer Denis Compton scores career best 278 in 287 mins against Pakistan at Nottingham. *Fun facts: Compton, posthumously inducted into the ICC Cricket Hall of Fame in 2009, is one of only twenty-five players to have scored over one hundred centuries in first-class cricket.*

4th July: Fourteen years of food rationing in Britain comes to an end when restrictions on the sale and purchase of meat are lifted. Members of the London Housewives' Association hold a special ceremony in London's Trafalgar Square to mark Derationing Day, and the Minister of Fuel and Power, Geoffrey Lloyd, burns a large replica of a ration book at an open meeting in his constituency. *Photo: A butcher advertises the end of meat rationing in Barnsley, South Yorkshire.*

5th	The BBC broadcasts its very first daily television news programme. Introduced by Richard Baker, the 20-minute bulletin begins with news of truce talks being held in Vietnam.
7th	British runner Jim Peters, 17 minutes ahead of any rival, collapses on the final stadium lap of the Commonwealth Games marathon in Vancouver. He is stretchered off and never races again.
10th	Sir Gordon Richards, considered by many to be the world's greatest ever jockey, breaks his pelvis and four ribs after being thrown off his horse in the paddock at Sandown Park. The fall enforces his retirement. *Fun facts: Richards was the British flat racing Champion Jockey 26 times and had a record 4,870 winning rides.*
15th	At the British Grand Prix Argentine driver Juan Manuel Fangio sets Silverstone's fastest ever lap, breaking the 100-mph barrier with a lap of 100.35-mph.
15th	The prolific artist of saucy seaside postcards, Donald McGill, is found guilty of breaching the Obscene Publications Act 1857 in Lincoln. The verdict sees McGill fined £10 and half a million of his postcards destroyed.

JUL

19th	The United Kingdom Atomic Energy Authority (UKAEA) is established with powers to produce, use and dispose of atomic energy, and to carry out research into this and any related matters.
20th	Crichel Down affair: A political scandal over compulsory land purchase leads to resignation of Sir Thomas Dugdale, the government minister responsible.
29th	The Fellowship of the Ring, the first of three volumes in J.R.R. Tolkien's epic fantasy novel "The Lord of the Rings" is published in the United Kingdom by George Allen & Unwin.
30th	The opening ceremony for the 5th British Empire Games and Commonwealth Games takes place in Vancouver, Canada.

AUG

3rd	No.1321 Flight RAF reforms at Wittering as a Vickers Valiant unit to integrate Blue Danube into service (the first operational British nuclear weapon).

4th August: The maiden flight of the English Electric Lightning P-1 supersonic fighter plane, piloted by Roland Beamont, takes place at Boscombe Down. *Fun facts: Further development led to the Lightning being capable of exceeding Mach 2.0, which it first achieved on the 25th November 1958. It was introduced into frontline service in 1960 and in total 337 of the aircraft (including prototypes) were built. The Lightning was retired by the RAF in 1988 after nearly three decades of service. Photo: Roland Beamont piloting the English Electric Lightning P.1A WG760 on its maiden flight.*

5th	Julian Slade's musical Salad Days opens at the Vaudeville Theatre in London's West End following its premiere at the Bristol Old Vic. *Notes: Salad Days would become the longest-running musical in British theatre history with 2,283 performances; today Agatha Christie's The Mousetrap holds that record with 28,735 performances.*

SEP

3rd	The National Trust for Scotland acquires Fair Isle (situated between Shetland and Orkney) with plans to expand research into migratory bird life.

SEP

11th	Roy of the Rovers first appears as a weekly feature in the comic magazine Tiger, debuting on the front page of the first issue.
14th	Benjamin Britten's chamber opera "The Turn of the Screw" receives its world premiere at the Teatro La Fenice in Venice, Italy.
15th	The Wolfenden Committee, set up to report on "Homosexual Offences and Prostitution", convenes for the first time. *Follow up: The committee's report is published on the 4th September 1957 and recommends that "homosexual behaviour between consenting adults in private should no longer be a criminal offence". The recommendations eventually lead to the passage of the Sexual Offences Act 1967 which permits homosexual acts between two consenting adults over the age of 21.*
17th	William Golding's debut novel "Lord of the Flies" is published by Faber and Faber in London. *Notes: A 2016 U.K. poll saw Lord of the Flies ranked third in the nation's favourite books from school behind George Orwell's Animal Farm and Charles Dickens' Great Expectations.*
18th	A marble head of the god of Mithras is unearthed during the excavation of a Roman Temple in Walbrook Square, London.
18th	The Last Night of the Proms for the first time features the coupling of Sir Henry Wood's 1905 "Fantasia on British Sea Songs", Sir Edward Elgar's 1902 setting of "Land of Hope and Glory", Sir Hubert Parry's 1916 setting of William Blake's "Jerusalem", and "Rule, Britannia!".
20th	The Silver Pears Trophy, presented annually by Pears Cyclopaedia for "outstanding British achievement in any field", is awarded to Roger Bannister.

28th September: A dispute over rates paid for handling meat cargoes results in an unofficial strike at London Docks. *Follow up: The National Amalgamated Stevedores and Dockers union declare an official strike from the 4th October. The strike spreads as other unions come out in sympathy. At its peak 43,500 workers are on strike leaving some 340 ships laying idle. The industrial action ends on the 1st November but further walk outs ensue as the dockers protests continue. Photo: London dock workers' delegate Victor Marney addresses a crowd of dockers at Lord Street, Liverpool, who ultimately decide to strike in support of their London comrades (19th October 1954).*

OCT

1st | The British colony of Nigeria becomes a federation under Governor-General John Stuart Macpherson.

13th | Chris Chataway, aged 23, breaks the world record for the 5000 metres by five seconds at White City athletics stadium in West London. Chataway records a time of 13m:51.6s, beating European champion Vladimir Kuts after a nail-biting finish in the London v Moscow match.

14th October: Ethiopian Emperor Haile Selassie begins his state visit to the United Kingdom. Accompanied by the Duke of Harar, he arrives aboard HMS Gambia in Portsmouth and travels by train to Victoria Railway station in London where he is met by the Queen, the Duke of Edinburgh, the Queen Mother, Princess Margaret, the Princess Royal and the Duchess of Gloucester. A carriage procession then conveys the Emperor and his suite to Buckingham Palace where he is to stay during his visit. *Photo: The Queen and Prince Philip ride in an open landau carriage with Emperor Haile Selassie at the start of his state visit (14th October 1954).*

19th | The Suez Canal Base Agreement between the United Kingdom and Egypt is signed at Cairo. The agreement replaces the Anglo-Egyptian Treaty of 1936 and provides for the gradual evacuation, and end to Britain's military occupation, of the Suez Canal.

NOV

2nd | The BBC radio comedy series Hancock's Half Hour, written by Ray Galton and Alan Simpson, is broadcast for the first time. The program stars Tony Hancock as Anthony Aloysius St John Hancock, a down-at-heel comedian living at the dilapidated 23, Railway Cuttings in East Cheam.

NOV

11th	The Two Towers, the second volume of J.R.R. Tolkien's novel "The Lord of the Rings" is published in the United Kingdom by George Allen & Unwin.

13th November: Great Britain defeats France 16-12 to capture the first ever Rugby League World Cup. *Photo: Great Britain's captain Dave Valentine holds aloft the inaugural Rugby League World Cup trophy in front of 30,368 spectators at the Parc des Princes in Paris.*

13th	BBC Television broadcasts the opening episode of "Fabian of the Yard", the first British police crime drama series. Starring Bruce Seton, the show is based on the real-life memoirs of Scotland Yard detective Robert Fabian.
24th	The Cohen Committee Court of Inquiry, established to examine the de Havilland Comet airline disasters, concludes that metal fatigue was the most likely cause of the two most recent crashes.
27th	During a hurricane-force storm the South Goodwin Lightship is wrecked on Goodwin Sands off the Deal coast in Kent; six of the seven men on board are lost.
29th	The case of Ladd v Marshall is decided in the Court of Appeal, establishing the criteria for the Court to admit fresh evidence in a case on which a judgement has already been delivered.

DEC

10th	The German-British physicist and mathematician Max Born, who was instrumental in the development of quantum mechanics, wins the 1954 Nobel Prize in Physics (shared with German nuclear physicist Walther Bothe).
25th	A BOAC Boeing 377 Stratocruiser crashes in poor visibility when landing at Prestwick Airport in Scotland; 28 of the 36 on board are killed.

Worldwide News & Events

1. 3rd January: Radiotelevisione Italiana (RAI), the national public broadcasting company of Italy, begins transmitting a regular television service.
2. 4th January: During a demo session at Sun Records' Studio in Memphis, Tennessee, an 18-year-old Elvis Presley records "I'll Never Stand in Your Way" / "It Wouldn't Be the Same Without You". *Notes: This was the second demo Elvis made; the first was "My Happiness" / "That's When Your Heartaches Begin" on the 18th July 1953. Presley reportedly gave this first acetate to his mother as a much-belated extra birthday present, although many biographers suggest that Presley simply wanted to get noticed by Sun owner Sam Phillips (these suggestions are strengthened by the fact that the Presleys did not own a record player at the time).*
3. 11th January: Two large avalanches strike the village of Blons, western Austria, within 9 hours of each other. The second buries rescue workers who are attempting to save civilians from the first avalanche; 125 people are killed and 55 houses / hundreds of farm buildings are destroyed.

4. 14th January: Actress, model and singer Marilyn Monroe marries baseball legend Joe DiMaggio at San Francisco City Hall in California. *Photo: Monroe and DiMaggio, surrounded by journalists, exit City Hall after their brief wedding ceremony.*

5. 15th January: The Mau Mau leader Waruhiu Itote is captured in Kenya and charged with consorting with persons carrying firearms, and being in possession of ammunition. Itote is found guilty and sentenced to hang but agrees to cooperate with the government (to negotiate an end to the uprising) in return for his life.
6. 16th January: In Yugoslavia, Milovan Djilas, one of the leading members of the League of Communists of Yugoslavia, is relieved of his duties.

7. 16th January: Richard Rodgers and Oscar Hammerstein's musical "South Pacific" closes at the Majestic Theater on Broadway after 1925 performances. *Fun facts: When it closed it was the second-longest-running musical in Broadway history after Oklahoma! The production won ten Tony Awards including Best Musical, Best Score and Best Libretto, and is the only musical production to win Tony Awards in all four acting categories.*

8. 21st January: The world's first operational nuclear-powered submarine, the USS Nautilus, is launched into the Thames River by America's First Lady Mamie Eisenhower at Groton, Connecticut. *Fun fact: On the 3rd August 1958, the Nautilus became the first submarine to complete a submerged transit of the North Pole. Photo: Crowds look on as USS Nautilus is launched.*

9. 22nd January: The 11th Golden Globe Awards, honouring the best in film for 1953, are held at the Club Del Mar in Santa Monica, California. The winners include "The Robe" (directed by Henry Koster), Spencer Tracy and Audrey Hepburn.

10. 11th February: The 6th (Primetime) Emmy Awards, to honour the best in American television, are held at the Hollywood Palladium in Los Angeles, California. Hosted by president of the Academy of Television Arts and Sciences, Don DeFore, the winners include "I Love Lucy" (Best Situation Comedy), Donald O'Connor (Best Male Star) and Eve Arden (Best Female Star).

11. 18th February: Incorporation papers are filed in Los Angeles for the Church of Scientology of California, the first official Scientologist organisation.

12. 19th February: The province of Crimea is gifted to the Ukrainian Soviet Socialist Republic by Russian Premier Nikita Khrushchev.

13. 19th February: At the World Figure Skating Championships in Oslo, Norway, the men's competition is won by defending champion Hayes Alan Jenkins of the United States, and the women's competition is won by Gundi Busch of West Germany.

14. 23rd February: The first mass vaccination of children against polio (paralytic poliomyelitis) begins at Arsenal Elementary School in Pittsburgh, Pennsylvania. *Follow up: The results of the trials announced in 1955 show that the new polio vaccine, developed by Dr. Jonas Salk at the Virus Research Lab at the University of Pittsburgh, is 80-90% effective at preventing polio.*

15. 1st March: The United States carries out its largest ever nuclear detonation "Castle Bravo" at Bikini Atoll in the Marshall Islands. *NB: Serious miscalculations by designers saw the explosive energy from the bomb reach 15 megatons, two and a half times what was expected. The mushroom cloud climbed up to roughly 25 miles and an area of 7,000 square miles was contaminated. Castle Bravo was approximately 1,000 times more powerful than the "Little Boy" atomic bomb detonated over Hiroshima during World War II. Photo: Nuclear weapon test Bravo on Bikini Atoll, part of Operation Castle.*

16. 1st March: Four Puerto Rican nationalists open fire in the United States House of Representatives chamber and wound five people. The assailants, seeking to promote the cause of Puerto Rico's independence from U.S. rule, are immediately apprehended by security guards.

17. 13th March: Viet Minh communist revolutionaries, under General Võ Nguyên Giáp, begin a massive artillery bombardment on the French Union's colonial Far East Expeditionary Corps, beginning the Battle of Dien Bien Phu. *Follow up: The Battle of Dien Bien Phu ends on the 7th May 1954 with a serious defeat for the French. It is the decisive battle of the First Indochina War.*

18. 16th March: The Army-McCarthy hearings, a series of televised hearings held by the United States Senate's Subcommittee on Investigations into conflicting accusations between the U.S. Army and Senator Joseph McCarthy, are convened. *NB: The media coverage greatly contributes to McCarthy's decline in popularity and his eventual censure by the Senate on the 2nd December 1954.*

19. 22nd March: The Northland Center shopping mall opens in in Southfield, Michigan. Designed by Victor Gruen and built at a cost of $30,000,000, it is (at the time) the world's largest shopping center.

20. 23rd March: The Soviet Union declares that it will establish diplomatic relations with the German Democratic Republic (East Germany).

21. 25th March: The 26th Academy Awards ceremony is simultaneously held at RKO Pantages Theatre in Hollywood (hosted by Donald O'Connor) and NBC Century Theatre in New York City (hosted by Fredric March). Fred Zinnemann's "From Here to Eternity" wins eight awards matching the record set by Gone with the Wind (1939). The Best Actor / Actress Awards go to William Holden and Audrey Hepburn. *Photos: Oscar winners Audrey Hepburn and William Holden.*

22. 28th March: The 8th Annual Tony Awards, presented by the American Theatre Wing, take place at the Plaza Hotel Grand Ballroom in New York City. Hosted by James Sauter the winners include "Teahouse of the August Moon" (Best Play), "Kismet" (Best Musical), David Wayne (Distinguished Dramatic Actor) and Audrey Hepburn (Distinguished Dramatic Actress).

23. 28th March: The trial of A. L. Zissu and 12 other Zionist leaders ends with harsh sentences in Communist Romania.

24. 30th March: The Yonge Street Subway, the first operational subway line in Canada, opens in Toronto.

25. 1st April: President Eisenhower signs Public Law 325, an Act of Congress establishing the United States Air Force Academy. A commission to select a site for the Academy is appointed by Secretary of the Air Force Harold E. Talbot and, after reviewing 582 proposed locations, Colorado Springs, Colorado, is chosen on the 24th June 1954.

26. 3rd April: Russian spy Vladimir Petrov, who was masquerading as a diplomat in Canberra, Australia, defects from the Soviet Union and asks for political asylum. *NB: The defection and subsequent information that Petrov passed onto Australian authorities had global implications through the identification of spy networks around the world.*

27. 4th April: Legendary symphony conductor Arturo Toscanini experiences a lapse of memory during a concert broadcast live from Carnegie Hall. The following day his retirement is announced and he never conducts in public again.

28. 8th April: A Royal Canadian Air Force Canadair Harvard collides with a Trans-Canada Air Lines Canadair North Star over Moose Jaw, Saskatchewan; 37 people are killed.

29. 9th April: The 7th Cannes Film Festival comes to a close. The Japanese film "Gate of Hell" wins the Grand Prix du Festival International du Film.

30. 11th April: The most boring day of the 20th century. *Notes: In November 2010, True Knowledge, an answer engine developed by William Tunstall-Pedoe in Cambridge, England, used some 300 million facts to calculate that Sunday, 11th April 1954, was the most boring day since 1900.*

31. 12th April: Bill Haley and His Comets record "Rock Around the Clock" in their first session for Decca at Pythian Temple studios in New York City; the record is released on the 20th May as the B-side to "Thirteen Women (and Only One Man in Town)". *NB: The song took off after its inclusion in the movie Blackboard Jungle (1955), and became the first rock and roll recording to top of the American Billboard chart on the 9th July 1955.*

32. 13th April: A hearing by the U.S. Atomic Energy Commission into Robert Oppenheimer's security clearance begins after he was accused of being a communist. *Follow up: Oppenheimer's clearance is revoked by the panel on the 27th May 1954, which ends his role in government and policy. Notes: During the Manhattan Project, Oppenheimer was director of the Los Alamos Laboratory and responsible for the research and design of the atomic bomb.*

33. 22nd April: The 1951 United Nations "Convention Relating to the Status of Refugees" comes into force, defining the status of refugees and setting out the basis for granting right of asylum.

34. 25th April: Bell labs announces the invention of the first practical silicon solar cell in Murray Hill, New Jersey. About 6% efficient, they demonstrate their solar panel by using it to power a toy Ferris wheel (pictured) and a solar powered radio transmitter.

35. 26th April: An international conference on Korea and Indochina opens in Geneva.

36.	26th April: Akira Kurosawa's epic film "Seven Samurai" is released in Japan.
37.	1st May: The Unification Church is founded in Seoul, South Korea, by Sun Myung Moon. A new religious movement derived from Christianity, the church's members are called Unificationists (or informally Moonies).
38.	3rd May: The Pulitzer Prize for Autobiography / Biography is awarded to Charles A. Lindbergh for "The Spirit of St. Louis".
39.	4th May: General Alfredo Stroessner leads a military coup in Paraguay, overthrowing the government of President Federico Chávez. *NB: Stroessner became President of Paraguay on the 15th August 1954 and remained in office until the 3rd February 1989.*
40.	8th May: The Asian Football Confederation (AFC) is formed in Manila, Philippines. *Notes: The AFC is the governing body of association football in Asia and Australia.*
41.	8th May: Parry O'Brien becomes the first shot putter to venture beyond the 60ft mark, throwing 60ft 5¼in (18.42m) at the Los Angeles Coliseum in California.
42.	14th May: The Hague Convention for the "Protection of Cultural Property in the Event of Armed Conflict" is adopted in The Hague, Netherlands.
43.	17th May: A landmark decision by the U.S. Supreme Court, in the case of Brown v. Board of Education of Topeka, rules that segregated schools are unconstitutional.
44.	22nd May: The Common Nordic Labor Market Act comes into effect allowing citizens of any Scandinavian country to work freely within the region.
45.	24th May: The Viking 11 sounding rocket attains an altitude of 158 miles at White Sands Missile Range in New Mexico (a record for a Western single-stage rocket at that time).
46.	26th May: A fire and series of explosions on board the American aircraft carrier USS Bennington, off Narragansett Bay, Massachusetts, kills 103 sailors.

47. 28th May: U.S. Air Force test pilot Major Arthur W. "Kit" Murray pilots the Bell X-1A rocket plane to record altitude of 27,570m. He flies high enough that the sky darkens and he is able to see the curvature of the Earth - newspapers call him "America's first space pilot". *Photo: Murray with the Bell X-1A rocket plane at Edwards AFB (20th July 1954).*

48. 29th May: In Australia Robert Menzies' Liberal / Country Coalition Government is re-elected with a decreased majority, defeating the Labor Party led by H.V. Evatt.
49. 29th May: The first of the annual Bilderberg conferences, fostering relations between Europe and North America, are held at the Hotel de Bilderberg in Oosterbeek, Netherlands.
50. 30th May: Czech long-distance runner Emile Zatopek runs a world record 5,000m (13m:57.2s) in Paris. Two days later in Brussels he becomes the first person to run 10,000m in under 29 minutes (28m:54.2s). *Fun facts: Zatopek is the only person to have won the 5,000 metres, 10,000 metres, and Marathon, at the same Olympic Games (Helsinki 1952).*
51. 2nd June: A general election in Ireland sees John A. Costello (Fine Gael) elected Taoiseach for the second time.
52. 6th June: The Eurovision television network makes its first broadcast, a live transmission from the Narcissus Festival in Montreux, Switzerland. *Notes: The transmission was relayed simultaneously in Belgium, Denmark, France, Germany, Italy, the Netherlands and the United Kingdom.*
53. 6th June: A Statue of Yuriy Dolgorukiy, commemorating the founding of Moscow in 1147 by Yuriy Dolgorukiy, is erected in a solemn ceremony opposite Moscow City Hall.
54. 14th June: President Eisenhower signs a bill to insert the phrase "under God" into the American Pledge of Allegiance.
55. 15th June: UEFA, the Union of European Football Associations, is formed in Basel, Switzerland.
56. 17th June: Rocky Marciano beats Ezzard Charles in a unanimous points decision in his third world heavyweight boxing title defense at Yankee Stadium in New York City. *Notes: A rematch between the two fighters on the 17th September 1954 saw Marciano victorious once again after he knocked out Charles in 2m:36s of the 8th round.*
57. 18th June: In France, Pierre Mendès forms a government with support from the centre-right. *NB: Mendès immediately negotiates an agreement with Ho Chi Minh, the Vietnamese Communist leader, aimed at ending the Indochina War.*
58. 19th June: The animated cartoon character the Tasmanian Devil (commonly referred to as Taz) makes his debut alongside Bugs Bunny in the Looney Tunes short "Devil May Hare".
59. 22nd June: Pauline Parker, 16, and her friend Juliet Hulme, 15, bludgeon Parker's mother to death using a brick at Victoria Park in New Zealand. *Follow up: Parker and Hulme are convicted of murder on the 28th August 1954 and, as they are too young to be considered for the death penalty, each spend five years in prison.*
60. 26th June: The Obninsk Nuclear Power Plant, the first grid-connected nuclear power plant in the world, is commissioned in the Soviet Union.
61. 27th June: The democratically elected Guatemalan president, Jacobo Árbenz, is deposed as a result of a CIA-sponsored military coup (code-named PBSuccess).
62. 27th June: A FIFA World Cup quarter-final match between Hungary and Brazil descends into an all-out brawl. The ill-temper continues after the game with the Brazilian players invading the Hungarian dressing room and continuing the on-pitch fighting. *Notes: During the "Battle of Berne", in which Hungary beat Brazil 4-2, there were 42 free kicks, 2 penalties, 4 cautions and 3 dismissals.*
63. 29th June: The 4th Berlin International Film Festival comes to a close. The Golden Bear is won by David Lean for his film "Hobson's Choice".
64. 4th July: West Germany beats the heavily favoured Golden Team of Hungary 3-2 to win the 1954 FIFA World Cup at Wankdorf Stadium in Bern, Switzerland. *Fun fact: Earlier in the group stage Hungary had defeated West Germany 8-3.*

65. 5th July: Elvis Presley's tapes his first professional recording session at Sam Phillips' Memphis Sun Studios. The session, featuring Elvis on acoustic guitar and vocals, Bill Black on double bass, and Scotty Moore on lead guitar, produces their historic cover of Arthur "Big Boy" Crudup's song "That's All Right". The song is released on the 19th July 1954, with "Blue Moon of Kentucky" on the B-side. Both sides of the record are wildly popular in Memphis prompting Phillips to send Elvis out on the road to promote the record. *Follow up: In total Elvis recorded a further 18 songs with Sun Records (not all were released) before Phillips announced that he had sold Elvis's recording contract to RCA Records in November 1955. Photo: Scotty Moore, Elvis and Bill Black on a weekly broadcast of "Louisiana Hayride" at the Shreveport Auditorium (16th October 1954).*

66. 15th July: The quadjet prototype aircraft Boeing 367-80 (or Dash 80) makes its maiden flight. *Notes: The Dash 80 would serve as basis for the design of Boeing's KC-135 tanker and its 707 airliner.*
67. 16th July: Groundbreaking begins on the Disneyland theme park in Anaheim, California. *Notes: Disneyland opened to invited guests and the media a year and a day later on the 17th July 1955; it opened to the public the following day.*
68. 20th July: The 1954 Geneva Conference, intended to settle outstanding issues resulting from the Korean War and the First Indochina War, closes in Switzerland. Three agreements regarding French Indochina, covering Cambodia, Laos and Vietnam, are signed on the 21st July 1954 and take effect two days later.
69. 31st July: Italian mountaineers Lino Lacedelli and Achille Compagnoni become the first to reach the summit of the world's second highest mountain, K2, in the Karakoram mountain range. *Notes: K2 (8,611m / 28,251ft) is notably more difficult to climb than the world's highest peak Mount Everest (8,849m / 29,032ft).*
70. 1st August: The South African Natives Resettlement Act comes into being, empowering the South African Government to remove black Africans from any area within and next to the magisterial district of Johannesburg.

71. 1st August: Louison Bobet of France wins the 41st Tour de France. The race, contested over 23 stages (2,893 miles), saw Bobet take the second of his three consecutive wins.

72. 6th August: 20-year-old Emilie Dionne, one of the Dionne quintuplets, dies of asphyxiation following an epileptic seizure at a convent in Sainte Agathe, Canada. *NB: The Dionne Quintuplets were internationally famous for being the first known quintuplets to have survived their infancy. Photo: The Dionne Quintuplets on their fourth birthday. From left: Emilie, Annette, Marie, Cecile and Yvonne (28th May 1938).*

73. 22nd August: Juan Manuel Fangio of Argentina clinches his second Formula 1 World Drivers Championship by winning Swiss Grand Prix at Bremgarten.

74. 23rd August: The Lockheed C-130 Hercules, a four-engine turboprop military transport aircraft, makes its first flight at Burbank, California, piloted by Stanley Beltz and Roy Wimmer. *Fun fact: The C-130 is the world's longest continuously produced military aircraft (1954-present).*

75. 24th August: Brazilian president Getúlio Vargas commits suicide after being accused of involvement in a conspiracy to murder his chief political opponent Carlos Lacerda.

76. 24th August: President Eisenhower signs the Communist Control Act outlawing the Communist Party of the United States and, amongst other things, prohibiting members of Communist organisations from serving in certain representative capacities.

77. 31st August: Hurricane Carol makes landfall on eastern Long Island, New York, and then over eastern Connecticut, with sustained winds estimated at 110-mph. *Notes: Hurricane Carol results in the deaths of 72 people and causes damage totalling $462 million (equivalent to $5.25 billion in 2023). It was the costliest hurricane in the history of the United States at the time.*

78. 7th September: Integration begins at public schools in Washington, D.C. and Baltimore, Maryland, after the United States Supreme Court's unanimous 9-0 decision on the 17th May ruling that "separate educational facilities are inherently unequal".

79.	7th September: The 15th Venice International Film Festival comes to a close. The Golden Lion is awarded to Renato Castellani's adaptation of William Shakespeare's play "Romeo and Juliet".
80.	8th September: The Southeast Asia Treaty Organization (SEATO) is signed in Manila, Philippines, by the United States, France, Great Britain, New Zealand, Australia, the Philippines, Thailand and Pakistan. Its primary objective is to prevent communism from gaining ground in the region.
81.	9th September: An earthquake shakes Orléansville (now named Chlef) in northern Algeria, leaving over 1,243 people dead and approximately 5,000 injured. The shock measures 6.7 on the moment magnitude scale and has a maximum Mercalli intensity of XI (Extreme).
82.	9th September: "On the Waterfront", starring Marlon Brando and Eva Marie Saint, premieres in London (the film wins 8 Oscars at the 1955 Academy Awards).
83.	14th September: The Soviet Union carries out the Totskoye nuclear exercise to explore defensive and offensive warfare during nuclear war.
84.	18th September: Finnish president J. K. Paasikivi becomes the first Western head of state to be awarded the highest honour of the Soviet Union, the Order of Lenin.
85.	20th September: The Constitution of the People's Republic of China is adopted and enacted through the first session of the First National People's Congress in Beijing.
86.	26th September: The Japanese ferry Tōya Maru sinks during Typhoon Marie in the Tsugaru Strait. Of the 1,309 people on board, 1,159 of them are killed.
87.	27th September: The Tonight Show, hosted by Steve Allen, premieres on NBC television in the United States. *Fun fact: Still broadcast today, The Tonight Show is the world's longest-running talk show.*
88.	29th September: CERN (the European Organisation for Nuclear Research) is founded by Belgium, Denmark, France, West Germany, Greece, Italy, the Netherlands, Norway, Sweden, Switzerland, the United Kingdom, and Yugoslavia.
89.	30th September: "The Boy Friend", starring Julie Andrews in her Broadway debut, opens at the Royale Theatre in New York City. *Notes: For her "outstanding New York City stage debut performance" Andrew's received the Theatre World Award.*
90.	5th October: Hurricane Hazel, the deadliest, second-costliest, and most intense hurricane of the 1954 Atlantic hurricane season, forms. It dissipates on the 18th October by which time it has killed at least 469 people in Haiti, 95 Americans and 81 Canadians.
91.	5th October: The 10th General Conference on Weights and Measures opens. *NB: Resolution 3 at the conference introduces a new internationally standardised Kelvin scale: 0°C = 273.15K.*
92.	9th October: Viet Minh soldiers arrive to take control of Hanoi, the capital city of French Indochina. The French military garrison lowers its flag for the last time and withdraws from the city.
93.	10th October: The 1st National Film Awards, to honour the best of Indian Cinema for the year 1953, takes place at Vigyan Bhavan, New Delhi. Presented by the President of India, Rajendra Prasad, "Shyamchi Aai" wins the Golden Lotus Award.
94.	12th October: Viet Minh leader Ho Chi Minh enters Hanoi without fanfare and takes up the reins of the government of North Vietnam.
95.	18th October: Industrial Development Engineering Associates, (I.D.E.A) of Indianapolis, Indiana, announce the Regency TR-1 transistor radio. Put on sale a month later using Texas Instruments NPN transistors, the Regency TR-1 is the first commercially manufactured transistor radio.
96.	19th October: Josef Jöchler and Herbert Tichy of Austria, and Sherpa Pasang Dawa Lama of India, make the first ascent of Cho Oyu, the sixth highest mountain in the world (8,188m / 26,863ft).

97.	25th October: Landslides, caused by heavy rains, hit the villages of Vietri sul Mare and Maiori off the Amalfi Coast, Italy; over 300 people are killed.
98.	26th October: Muslim Brotherhood member Mahmoud Abdul Latif tries to assassinate Gamal Abdel-Nasser, the prime minister of Egypt, at Manshiya Square in the Mediterranean city of Alexandria. *NB: Vengeance taken upon the Brotherhood was swift and harsh. The Muslim Brotherhood was banned and over 1,000 members were arrested. A small number of these were executed.*

99. 27th October: The first "Godzilla" film premieres in Nagoya, Japan. It is met with mixed reviews upon release but is a box-office success, winning the Japanese Movie Association Award for Best Special Effects. *Fun fact: The Godzilla franchise has been recognised by Guinness World Records as being the longest-running film franchise in history (36 films in total). Photo: Production still from the Japanese epic kaiju film Godzilla (1954).*

100.	27th October: Walt Disney's first television show "Disneyland" premieres on ABC. The show is an instant hit with audiences and sets the stage for a new era in American family entertainment.
101.	1st November: A series of 70 attacks, committed by militant members of the Algerian National Liberation Front (FLN), take place in French Algeria. *NB: This revolt against French rule is usually seen as the starting date for the Algerian War (which lasted until 1962 and led to Algerian independence from France).*
102.	7th November: A U.S. Air Force RB-29 Superfortress reconnaissance aircraft, on a routine photo mapping mission, is shot down by a pair of Soviet MiG-15 fighters near Hokkaido, Japan; 10 of the 11-crew land safely after bailing out, the eleventh drowns after getting tangled in his parachute lines after hitting the water.
103.	9th November: The treatment of Burma by the Japanese in WWII is settled by a peace treaty and reparations agreement signed by Burmese foreign minister, Kyaw Nyein, and Japanese foreign minister, Okazaki Katsuo, in Rangoon.

104. 12th November: The immigrant-detention center at Ellis Island in New York Harbor closes permanently with the departure of its last detainee, Norwegian merchant seaman Arne Pettersen who had been arrested for overstaying his shore leave. *Notes: Ellis Island was the busiest immigrant inspection and processing station in the United States. From 1892 to 1954, nearly 12 million immigrants arriving at the Port of New York and New Jersey were processed there under federal law.*
105. 22nd November: Berman v. Parker: The United States Supreme Court votes 8-0 to uphold federal slum clearance and urban renewal programs.
106. 23rd November: The Dow Jones Industrial Average rises 3.27 points, or 0.86%, closing at an all-time high of 382.74. More significantly, this is the first time the Dow has surpassed its previous peak of 381.17, reached on the 3rd September 1929, just before the Wall Street Crash.
107. 30th November: In Sylacauga, Alabama, a fragment of a meteorite crashes through the roof of a house and hits a woman who is napping on her couch. The badly bruised woman, a Mrs Ann Hodges, is the first ever documented individual to be struck by a meteorite.
108. 2nd December: The Sino-American Mutual Defense Treaty between the U.S. and Republic of China (Taiwan) is signed. *Notes: The treaty is intended to defend the island of Taiwan from invasion by the People's Republic of China.*

109. 10th December: Lt. Col. John Stapp travels at 632 mph aboard the Sonic Wind No.1 rocket sled at Holloman Air Force Base in New Mexico, breaking the land speed record and making him the fastest man on Earth. *Photo: The Holloman High Speed Test Track crew secures Lt. Col. John Stapp into the Sonic Wind No.1 rocket sled moments before he breaks the world land speed record.*

110. 11th December: The American USS Forrestal supercarrier is launched at Newport News, Virginia. *NB: The Forrestal was the largest aircraft carrier built to that date and was the first designed to support jet aircraft.*

111. 15th December: The Netherlands Antilles is created out of several Dutch island territories located in the Caribbean Sea.
112. 23rd December: The first successful kidney transplant is performed by Dr Joseph E. Murray at the Peter Bent Brigham Hospital in Boston, Massachusetts. The donor and recipient are identical twins Ronald and Richard Herrick who, because of their identical genetic make-ups, are able to avoid the issue of rejection by the recipient immune system. *NB: Dr Murray jointly received the Nobel Prize in Physiology or Medicine in 1990 alongside physician E. Donnall Thomas "for their discoveries concerning organ and cell transplantation in the treatment of human disease".*
113. 28th December: At the 43rd Davis Cup, the most important tournament between national teams in men's tennis, the United States defeats defending champions Australia in the Challenge Round. The 3-2 win, at White City Stadium in Sydney, Australia, ends Australia's four-year championship run.

BIRTHS

British Personalities

BORN IN 1954

Richard Gibson
b. 1st January 1954

Actor known for his role as Gestapo Officer Herr Otto Flick in the BBC sitcom 'Allo 'Allo!

Tom Bailey
b. 18th January 1954

Singer, songwriter, musician, composer and record producer (Thompson Twins).

Anthony Head
b. 20th February 1954

Actor and singer.

Willie Thorne
b. 4th March 1954
d. 17th June 2020
Snooker player and commentator.

Cheryl Baker
b. 8th March 1954

Singer and television presenter (Co-Co, Bucks Fizz, The Fizz).

David Wilkie, MBE
b. 8th March 1954

Swimmer who won gold at the 1976 Summer Olympics in Montreal.

Baroness **Valerie Amos**, LG, CH, PC
b. 13th March 1954

Labour Party politician and diplomat created a life peer in 1997.

Jimmy Nail
b. 16th March 1954

Singer-songwriter, actor, film producer and television writer.

Lesley-Anne Down
b. 17th March 1954

Actress, singer and model.

Sir **Iain Duncan Smith**
b. 9th April 1954

Politician who served as Leader of the Conservative Party from 2001 to 2003.

Trevor Francis
b. 19th April 1954
d. 24th July 2023
Britain's first £1 million football player who was capped 52 times for England.

Captain Sensible
b. 23rd April 1954

Singer, songwriter and guitarist born Raymond Ian Burns (The Damned).

Gary Wilmot, MBE
b. 8th May 1954

Singer, actor, comedian, presenter, writer and director.

Andy Hamilton
b. 28th May 1954

Comedian, game show panellist, director, screenwriter, dramatist, novelist and actor.

Anne Kirkbride
b. 21st June 1954
d. 19th January 2015
Actress who played Deirdre Barlow on ITV's Coronation Street for 42 years.

Neil Tennant
b. 10th July 1954

Singer, songwriter and music journalist (Pet Shop Boys).

Sammy McIlroy, MBE
b. 2nd August 1954

Football player and manager capped 88 times for Northern Ireland, 19 as captain.

Joe Jackson
b. 11th August 1954

Musician, singer and songwriter.

Elvis Costello, OBE
b. 25th August 1954

Songwriter, singer, record producer, author, television presenter and occasional actor.

Steve Wright
b. 26th August 1954

Radio personality, television presenter and disc jockey.

Mark Drakeford
b. 19th September 1954

Politician serving as First Minister of Wales and Leader of Welsh Labour since 2018.

Cherie Blair, CBE, KC
b. 23rd September 1954

Barrister and writer married to former Prime Minister Tony Blair.

Helen Lederer
b. 24th September 1954

Comedian, writer and actress.

Carole Malone
b. 14th October 1954

Television presenter, journalist and broadcaster.

Lee Child, CBE
b. 29th October 1954

Author, born James Dover Grant, best known for his Jack Reacher novel series.

Adam Ant
b. 3rd November 1954

Singer, musician and actor born Stuart Leslie Goddard.

Annie Lennox, OBE
b. 25th December 1954

Singer-songwriter, political activist and philanthropist.

Alex Salmond
b. 31st December 1954

SNP politician who served as First Minister of Scotland from 2007 to 2014.

Notable British Deaths

1st Jan	Alfred Duff Cooper, 1st Viscount Norwich, GCMG, DSO, PC (b. 22nd February 1890) - Conservative Party politician and diplomat who was also a military and political historian.
18th Jan	Sydney Hughes Greenstreet (b. 27th December 1879) - British-American actor best remembered for the three Warner Bros. films: The Maltese Falcon (1941), Casablanca (1942), and Passage to Marseille (1944).
20th Jan	Charles Frederick Root (b. 16th April 1890) - Cricketer who played for Derbyshire (1910-1920), Worcestershire (1921-1932), and England (1926).
1st Feb	Sir Henry Dudley Gresham Leveson Gower (b. 8th May 1873) - Cricketer who played first-class cricket for Oxford University (1893-1896), Surrey (1895-1920), and captained England in all 3 of his Test matches (1910).
8th Feb	Ronald Niel Stuart, VC, DSO, RD, RNR (b. 26th August 1886) - Merchant Navy commodore and Royal Navy captain who was highly commended following extensive and distinguished service at sea over a period of more than 35 years. During World War I he was awarded the Victoria Cross, the Distinguished Service Order, the French Croix de Guerre avec Palmes and the United States' Navy Cross for a series of daring operations he conducted while serving in the Royal Navy against the German U-boat campaign in the Atlantic.
26th Feb	William Ralph Inge, KCVO, FBA (b. 6th June 1860) - Author, Anglican priest, professor of divinity at Cambridge, and dean of St Paul's Cathedral, who was nominated for the Nobel Prize in Literature three times.
4th Mar	Noel Gay (b. 15th July 1898) - Composer of popular music during the 1930s and 40s, whose output comprised of 45 songs, and the music for 28 films and 26 London shows. Born Reginald Moxon Armitage, he is best known for the musical "Me and My Girl".
4th Mar	John Dalzell Kenworthy (b. 5th November 1858) - Internationally acclaimed artist, sculptor and writer.
6th Mar	Prince Charles Edward (b. Leopold Charles Edward George Albert; 19th July 1884) - Grandson of Queen Victoria and Prince Albert who from birth held the titles of Duke of Albany, Earl of Clarence, and Baron Arklow. Charles Edward was sent to Germany in his mid-teens where he unexpectedly inherited the throne of the Duchy of Saxe-Coburg and Gotha in the German Empire. *NB: During the First World War his support for his adoptive country led to him to be viewed with increased hostility and he ultimately lost all his British titles.*
14th Mar	Fred Herd (b. 26th November 1873) - Scottish professional golfer who in 1898 won the U.S. Open at Myopia Hunt Club in South Hamilton, Massachusetts.
18th Mar	Walter Mead (b. 1st April 1868) - Principal bowler for Essex during their first two decades in first-class county cricket.
26th Mar	James Peters (b. 7th August 1879) - Rugby union player and, later, a rugby league footballer. *NB: Peters was the first black player to play rugby union for England.*
28th Mar	Francis Brett Young (b. 29th June 1884) - Poet, playwright, composer, doctor and soldier.
4th Apr	Frederick Lonsdale (b. 5th February 1881) - Playwright known for his librettos to several successful musicals.

29th Apr	Kathleen Clarice Groom (née Cornwell; 11th March 1872) - Writer of short-stories and novels.
6th May	Bertie Charles Forbes (b. 14th May 1880) - Scottish-American financial journalist and author who founded Forbes magazine.
10th May	George Herbert Hirst (b. 7th September 1871) - Cricketer who played first-class cricket for Yorkshire County Cricket Club (1891-1921, 1929) and England (1897-1909). One of the best all-rounders of his time, Hirst completed the double of 1,000 runs and 100 wickets in an English cricket season 14 times.
23rd May	Hugh Richard Bromley-Davenport, OBE (b. 18th August 1870) - Cricketer who played first-class cricket for Cambridge University (1892-1893), Middlesex (1896-1898), and England (1896-1899).

7th June: Alan Mathison Turing, OBE, FRS (b. 23rd June 1912) - Mathematician, computer scientist, logician, cryptanalyst, philosopher and theoretical biologist who was highly influential in the development of theoretical computer science, and is widely considered to be the father of theoretical computer science and artificial intelligence.

During the Second World War Turing played a crucial role in cracking intercepted coded messages that enabled the Allies to defeat the Axis powers in many crucial engagements, including the Battle of the Atlantic.

9th Jun	Arthur Greenwood, CH (b. 8th February 1880) - Prominent Labour Politician (1922-1954) who served as Deputy Leader of the Labour Party (1935-1945) under Clement Attlee.
15th Jun	William Ewart Berry, 1st Viscount Camrose, DL (b. 23rd June 1879) - Newspaper publisher who made his fortune with the publication of the First World War magazine "The War Illustrated", which at its peak had a circulation of 750,000.
1st Jul	Phyllis Barry (b. Gertrude Phyllis Hillyard; 7th December 1908) - Actress who appeared in over 40 films (1925-1947).
11th Jul	Henry Valentine Knaggs (b. 14th February 1859) - Physician, anti-vaccinationist, naturopath and alternative health writer.
11th Aug	Murray Kinnell (b. 24th July 1889) - English-American actor who appeared in 71 films (1930-1937).
1st Sep	Hector William "Harry" Cording (b. 26th April 1891) - English-American actor perhaps best remembered for his roles in the films The Black Cat (1934) and The Adventures of Robin Hood (1938).
29th Sep	William John Gruffydd (b. 14th February 1881) - Welsh scholar, poet, writer and editor, and the last Member of Parliament to represent the University of Wales seat.
3rd Oct	Herbert Prior (b. 2nd July 1867) - Silent film actor who appeared in more than 260 films (1908-1934).
7th Oct	Benjamin Seebohm Rowntree, CH (b. 7th July 1871) - Sociological researcher, social reformer and industrialist known for his three studies of poverty in York (conducted in 1899, 1935 and 1951).
27th Oct	Sydney Horler (b. 18th July 1888) - Prolific novelist specialising in thrillers.
19th Nov	Walter Bartley Wilson (b. 3rd January 1870) - Lithographic artist and the founder of Cardiff City Football Club.

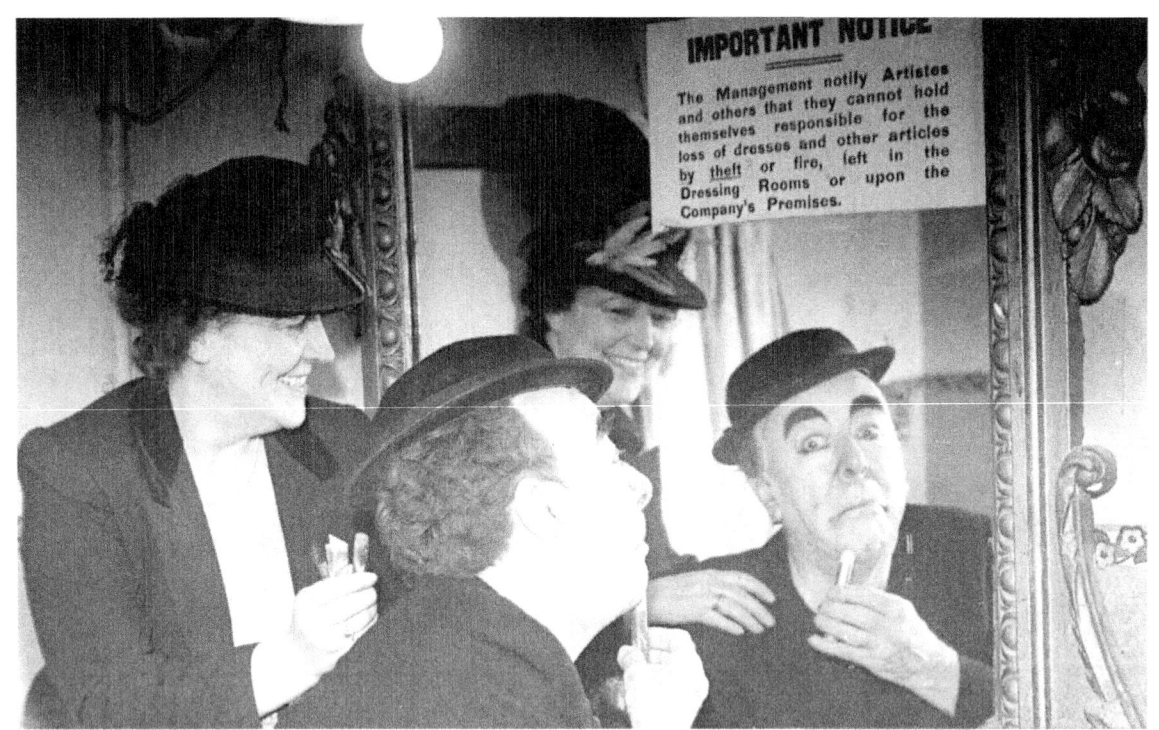

29th November: Sir George Edward Wade, CBE (b. 20th September 1869) - Comedian, singer and actor in musical theatre. Known professionally as George Robey, he was one of the greatest music hall performers of the late 19th and early 20th centuries. *Photo: Robey, the self-styled "Prime Minister of Mirth" (pictured with his wife Blanche), puts on his make-up prior to a show (circa 1945).*

20th Dec	James Hilton (b. 9th September 1900) - Novelist and screenwriter who is best remembered for his novels "Lost Horizon", "Goodbye, Mr. Chips" and "Random Harvest", as well as co-writing screenplays for the films Camille (1936) and Mrs. Miniver (1942), the latter earning him an Academy Award.

POPULAR MUSIC

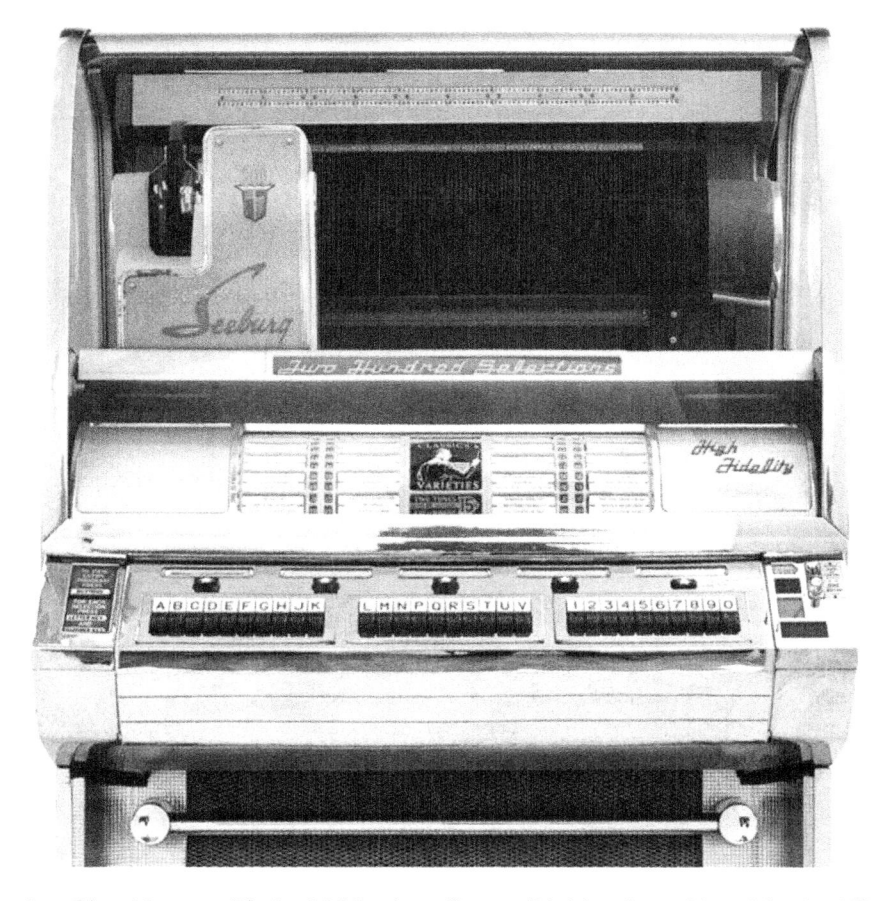

The U.K. Singles Chart began life in 1952 when Percy Dickins from New Musical Express (NME) imitated an idea started in American Billboard magazine and began compiling a hit parade. Prior to this, a song's popularity was measured by the sales of sheet music.

1954 No.1 Singles:

Date	Artist	Single
13-Nov-1953	Frankie Laine	Answer Me
08-Jan-1954	Eddie Calvert	Oh Mein Papa
12-Mar-1954	The Stargazers	I See the Moon
16-Apr-1954	Doris Day	Secret Love
23-Apr-1954	The Stargazers	I See the Moon
30-Apr-1954	Johnnie Ray	Such a Night
07-May-1954	Doris Day	Secret Love
02-Jul-1954	David Whitfield	Cara Mia
10-Sep-1954	Kitty Kallen	Little Things Mean a Lot
17-Sep-1954	Frank Sinatra	Three Coins in the Fountain
08-Oct-1954	Don Cornell	Hold My Hand
05-Nov-1954	Vera Lynn	My Son, My Son
19-Nov-1954	Don Cornell	Hold My Hand
26-Nov-1954	Rosemary Clooney	This Ole House
03-Dec-1954	Winifred Atwell	Let's Have Another Party

1954

The No.1 singles of 1954 are listed below and arranged by the number of weeks spent at the top of the U.K. Charts.

Artist	Single	Weeks
David Whitfield	Cara Mia	10
Doris Day	Secret Love	9
Eddie Calvert	Oh Mein Papa	9
The Stargazers	I See the Moon	6
Don Cornell	Hold My Hand	5
Winifred Atwell	Let's Have Another Party	4 (1954)
Frank Sinatra	Three Coins in the Fountain	3
Vera Lynn	My Son, My Son	2
Frankie Laine	Answer Me	1 (1954)
Johnnie Ray	Such a Night	1
Kitty Kallen	Little Things Mean a Lot	1
Rosemary Clooney	This Ole House	1

TOP 5 ARTISTS

1. David Whitfield

Label: Decca | Weeks at No.1: 10

David Whitfield (b. 2nd February 1925 - d. 15th January 1980) was a popular male tenor vocalist from Hull. During the 1950s he was the most successful British male singer in America, and was the first British male vocalist to earn a gold disc with his 1954 chart topper "Cara Mia". Recorded with **Annunzio Paolo Mantovani** (b. 15th November 1905 - d. 29th March 1980) and his Orchestra, "Cara Mia" ("my beloved" in Italian) went on to sell some three and a half million copies worldwide, was the first record to spend ten consecutive weeks at No.1 on the U.K. Singles Chart, and was one of the biggest selling British records of the pre-rock era.

② Doris Day

Label: Philips | **Weeks at No.1:** 9

Doris Day (b. 3rd April 1922 - d. 13th May 2019) was an actress, singer and animal rights activist. She began her career as a big band singer in 1939, and her popularity began to rise after her first hit recording, "Sentimental Journey", in 1945. During her solo career Day made more than 650 recordings and became one of the most popular singers of the 20th century.

---

③ Eddie Calvert

Label: Columbia | **Weeks at No.1:** 9

Albert Edward "Eddie" Calvert (b. 15th March 1922 - d. 7th August 1978) was a trumpeter who enjoyed his greatest success in the 1950s. Between 1953 and 1958, Calvert achieved seven instrumental hits on the U.K. Singles Chart, including two chart-toppers": "Oh, Mein Papa" in 1954 and "Cherry Pink (and Apple Blossom White)" in 1955.

4 The Stargazers

Label: Decca | **Weeks at No.1:** 6

The Stargazers were a British vocal group jointly founded in 1949 by Cliff Adams and Ronnie Milne (the other original members were Marie Benson, Fred Datchler and Dick James). Recording for Decca, The Stargazers enjoyed considerable commercial success during the 1950s, and had three U.K. No.1 hit singles, "Broken Wings", "I See the Moon", and "The Finger of Suspicion" (with Dickie Valentine).

5 Don Cornell

Label: Vogue | **Weeks at No.1:** 5

Don Cornell (b. Luigi Francisco Varlaro; 21st April 1919 - d. 23rd February 2004) was a singer and vocalist in the Sammy Kaye band from the age of eighteen. He became a solo act in 1949, and between 1950 and 1962, had twelve of his records certified gold. Cornell was inducted into the Big Band Hall of Fame in 1993.

1954: TOP FILMS

1. **Doctor in the House** - *Rank Organisation (highest grossing U.K.)*
2. **White Christmas** - *Paramount Pictures (highest grossing U.S.)*
3. **On the Waterfront** - *Columbia Pictures*
4. **The Country Girl** - *Paramount Pictures*
5. **Seven Brides for Seven Brothers** - *Metro-Goldwyn-Mayer*

OSCARS

Best Picture: On the Waterfront
Most Nominations: On the Waterfront (12)
Most Wins: On the Waterfront (8)

Oscar winners Marlon Brando (Best Actor) and Grace Kelly (Best Actress).

Best Director: Elia Kazan - *On the Waterfront*

Best Actor: Marlon Brando - *On the Waterfront*
Best Actress: Grace Kelly - *The Country Girl*
Best Supporting Actor: Edmond O'Brien - *The Barefoot Contessa*
Best Supporting Actress: Eva Marie Saint - *On the Waterfront*

The 27th Academy Awards, honouring the best in film for 1954, were presented on the 30th March 1955 at RKO Pantages Theatre in Hollywood, California, and NBC Century Theatre in New York City.

DOCTOR IN THE HOUSE

Directed by: Ralph Thomas - Runtime: 1h 32m

The trials and tribulations of medical student Simon Sparrow as he trains to be a doctor at St Swithin's Hospital in London.

Starring

Dirk Bogarde
b. 28th March 1921
d. 8th May 1999
Character:
Simon Sparrow

Muriel Pavlow
b. 27th June 1921
d. 19th January 2019
Character:
Nurse Joy Gibson

Kenneth More
b. 20th September 1914
d. 12th July 1982
Character:
Richard Grimsdyke

Trivia

Interesting Facts | "Doctor in the House" was the most popular box office film of 1954 in Great Britain. Its massive success spawned six sequels, and a television and radio series.

Robert Morley demanded a fee of fifteen thousand pounds when offered the part of Sir Lancelot Spratt. As this would have constituted nearly one-sixth of the film's proposed budget, the filmmakers instead hired James Robertson Justice at one-tenth the salary. Justice scored a great personal triumph as the irascible chief surgeon Sir Lancelot Spratt, and played the role again in five sequels.

Richard Gordon, the author of the book "Doctor in the House", has an uncredited cameo in the film as an anaesthetist.

Kenneth More won the 1954 Best British Actor BAFTA Award for his role as Richard Grimsdyke in this film.

Quotes | *Sir Lancelot Spratt:* You cut a patient; he bleeds until the processes of nature form a clot and stop it. This interval is known scientifically as the 'bleeding time'. You! What's the bleeding time?
Simon Sparrow: Ten past ten, sir.

Sir Lancelot Spratt: You can cut the patient's throat while he's under general anaesthetic and nobody'll mind, but if you leave anything inside it'll be in the Sunday papers in no time.

WHITE CHRISTMAS

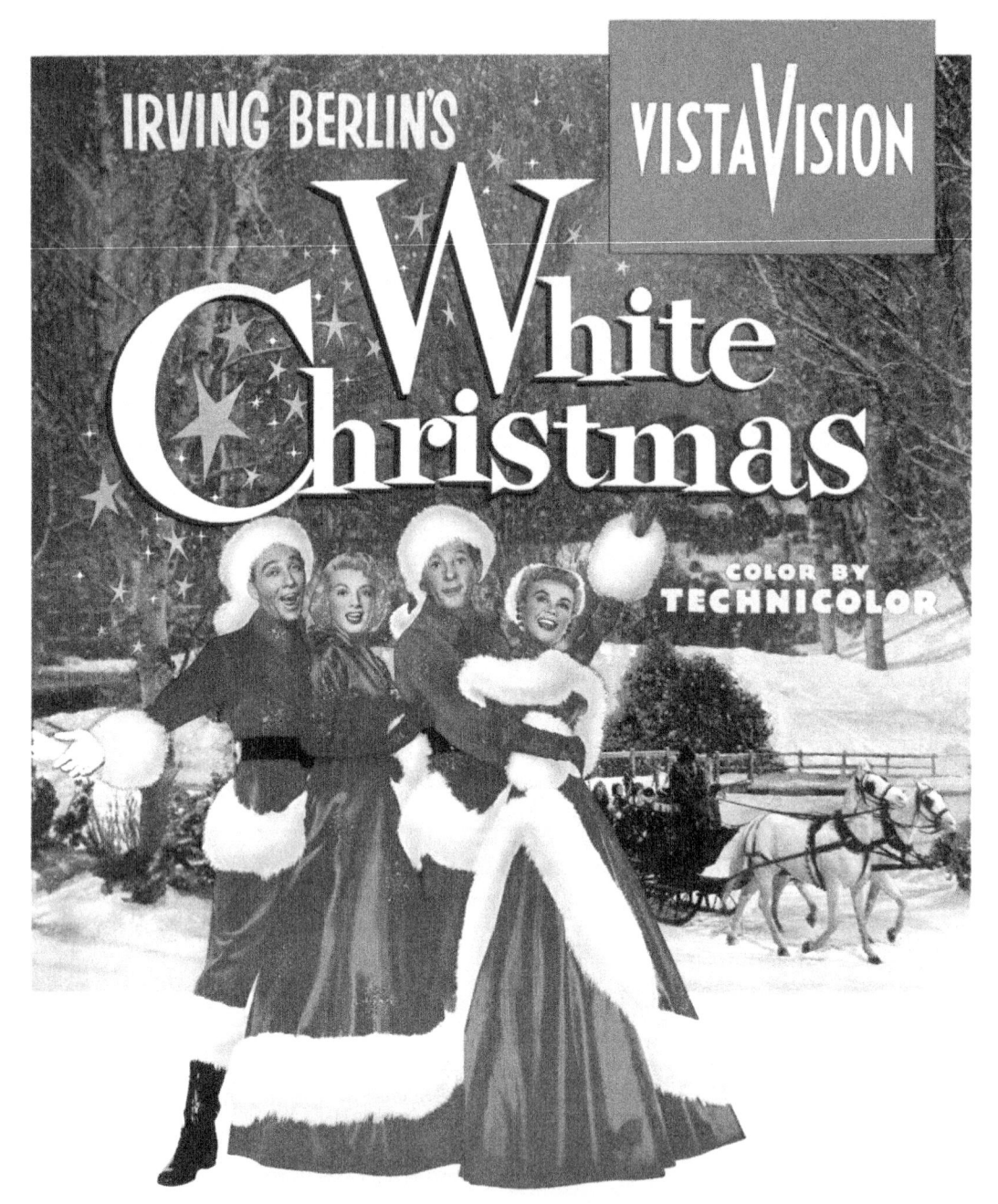

STARRING BING CROSBY · DANNY KAYE ROSEMARY CLOONEY · VERA-ELLEN

Directed by: Michael Curtiz - Runtime: 2h

A successful song-and-dance team become romantically involved with a sister act and team up to save the failing Vermont inn of their former commanding general.

Starring

Bing Crosby
b. 3rd May 1903
d. 14th October 1977
Character:
Bob Wallace

Danny Kaye
b. 18th January 1911
d. 3rd March 1987
Character:
Phil Davis

Rosemary Clooney
b. 23rd May 1928
d. 29th June 2002
Character:
Betty Haynes

Trivia

Goofs When the General appears in uniform at the inn his medals bars show his Purple Heart in first position and his Silver Star in second. These ribbons should be reversed, the Silver Star takes precedence over the Purple Heart.

The Columbia Inn Station Wagon that picks up Bob, Phil, Betty and Judy at the train station has a black and yellow California license plate - they are supposed to be in Vermont.

Interesting Facts According to Rosemary Clooney, Bing Crosby and Danny Kaye's "Sisters" performance was not originally in the script. They were clowning around on the set and director Michael Curtiz thought it was so funny that he decided to film it. In the scene Crosby's laughs are genuine and unscripted as he was unable to hold a straight face due to Kaye's comedic dancing.

Even though Betty was the elder of the Haynes sisters, Rosemary Clooney was actually seven years younger than Vera-Ellen in real life.

This was the third of three films to feature Bing Crosby singing "White Christmas". The other two are Holiday Inn (1942) and Blue Skies (1946).

Quote *Phil Davis:* My dear partner, when what's left of you gets around to what's left to be gotten, what's left to be gotten won't be worth getting, whatever it is you've got left.
Bob Wallace: When I figure out what that means I'll come up with a crushing reply.

ON THE WATERFRONT

Directed by: Elia Kazan - Runtime: 1h 48m

An ex-prize fighter turned New Jersey longshoreman struggles to stand up to his corrupt union bosses, including his older brother, as he starts to connect with the grieving sister of one of the syndicate's victims.

Starring

Marlon Brando
b. 3rd April 1924
d. 1st July 2004
Character:
Terry Malloy

Karl Malden
b. 22nd March 1912
d. 1st July 2009
Character:
Father Barry

Lee J. Cobb
b. 8th December 1911
d. 11th February 1976
Character:
Johnny Friendly

Trivia

Goofs | When Father Barry gets hit in the head with a beer can, he gets a cut on his forehead which bleeds visibly in the scene. In subsequent scenes there is no sign of the cut or of a bandage to show that he has been hurt.

In the final scene, the large ship at the dock in the background changes between a freighter and a cruise ship.

Interesting Facts | When producer Sam Spiegel originally sent the script to "On the Waterfront" to Marlon Brando it came back with a refusal. Spiegel, however, had inserted small pieces of paper between the pages which were still in place when the script was returned to him, indicating that it hadn't been read. While Spiegel continued to work on Brando, Frank Sinatra agreed to take on the role.

Although Eva Marie Saint's part of Edie Doyle is really a lead character in the film, producer Sam Spiegel listed her as a Supporting Actress in the hopes of getting her an Academy Award nomination. It worked and she won the Oscar for Best Actress in a Supporting Role.

Grace Kelly turned down the role of Edie Doyle, deciding to take the part of Lisa Carol Fremont in Alfred Hitchcock's Rear Window (1954) instead.

Quotes | *Terry:* Hey, you wanna hear my philosophy of life? Do it to him before he does it to you.

Terry: Conscience... that stuff can drive you nuts!

THE COUNTRY GIRL

Directed by: George Seaton - Runtime: 1h 44m

A director hires an alcoholic has-been and strikes up a stormy relationship with the actor's wife, who he believes is the cause of all the man's problems.

Starring

Bing Crosby
b. 3rd May 1903
d. 14th October 1977
Character:
Frank Elgin

Grace Kelly
b. 12th November 1929
d. 14th September 1982
Character:
Georgie Elgin

William Holden
b. 17th April 1918
d. 12th November 1981
Character:
Bernie Dodd

Trivia

Interesting Facts Bing Crosby initially turned down the role of Frank as he didn't want to play opposite what he considered a lesser actress. Grace Kelly's Oscar nomination for Best Supporting Actress for Mogambo (1953) helped change his mind and he was quickly won over by her dedication and professionalism during the making of the film.

Grace Kelly won her only Oscar for her role in this film beating Judy Garland, the sentimental favourite, in reportedly the closest Best Actress race in Academy history besides the Barbra Streisand and Katharine Hepburn tie in 1968.

Paramount was inundated with letters from "Catholic sources" complaining about Bing Crosby, a staunch Catholic, playing a drunk.

Bing Crosby proposed to Grace Kelly a short time after making this film but she turned him down. They would later star in High Society (1956) in which they play a divorced couple who remarry.

Quote *Bernie Dodd:* Does your wife really want you to play this part?
Frank Elgin: Yeah, she's all for it.
Bernie Dodd: I was just wondering. The day I met her, she seemed a little difficult about terms and rather domineering, I thought.
Frank Elgin: She wasn't always like that.
Bernie Dodd: Oh, I know, I know. They all start out as Juliets and wind up as Lady Macbeths.

SEVEN BRIDES FOR SEVEN BROTHERS

Directed by: Stanley Donen - Runtime: 1h 42m

In 1850 Oregon, a backwoodsman brings a wife home to his farm which, unbeknownst to her, he shares with his six brothers. She then sets out to reform the ill-mannered brothers and help them find wives of their own.

Starring

Jane Powell
b. 1st April 1929
d. 16th September 2021
Character:
Milly Pontipee

Howard Keel
b. 13th April 1919
d. 7th November 2004
Character:
Adam Pontipee

Jeff Richards
b. 1st November 1924
d. 28th July 1989
Character:
Benjamin Pontipee

Trivia

Goofs	When Adam is showing Milly the house, he opens the front door twice.
	In "Wonderful, Wonderful Day" birds fly onto the set and several crash into its painted backdrop.
Interesting Facts	MGM considered this a "B" picture and diverted some of its original budget to Brigadoon (1954) and Rose Marie (1954), which were expected to be the more successful films. This forced Stanley Donen to use painted backdrops instead of filming on location.
	For the brides' costumes, designer Walter Plunkett went to the Salvation Army, found old quilts and turned them into dresses.
	In order to distinguish them from the town suitors, MGM decided to make all the Pontipee Brothers red-headed.
	Howard Keel called this film "one of my happiest filmmaking experiences at Metro-Goldwyn-Mayer. The cast was magnificent, and the chemistry irresistible. Jack Cummings had his stamp on the whole picture. Jane Powell, as Milly, was perfect, and I loved working with her. She was cute and pernickety, and a multi-talented pro. It truly was one big happy family." In an interview for TNT's "Our Favorite Movies" series, Keel said, "A 'Seven Brides for Seven Brothers' doesn't come along too often. I remember thinking, 'If this isn't a hit, I give up,' because it was so much fun to make".
Quote	*Adam:* [sarcastically] May I escort you to the ball, ma'am?
Milly: Well, it wouldn't hurt you to learn some manners, too.
Adam: What do I need manners for? I already got me a wife.

SPORTING WINNERS

BBC SPORTS PERSONALITY OF THE YEAR

1954 BBC Sports Personality Awards: Christopher Chataway (left) and Roger Bannister.

1954	BBC Sports Personality Results	Country	Sport
Winner	**Christopher Chataway**	**England**	**Athletics**
Runner Up	Roger Bannister	England	Athletics
Third Place	Pat Smythe	England	Show Jumping

Christopher Chataway - Athletics

Sir **Christopher John Chataway** (b. 31st January 1931 - d. 19th January 2014) was a British middle- and long-distance runner, television news broadcaster, and Conservative Party politician.

Championship Medals:

Year	Competition	Medal	Event	Location
1954	European Championships	Silver	5000m	Bern
1954	British Empire & Commonwealth Games	Gold	3 miles	Vancouver

Chataway had a short but distinguished athletics career. When Roger Bannister ran the first sub-four-minute mile on the 6th May 1954, he was one of his pacemakers. Chataway finished in second place in the 5000m at the 1954 European Athletics Championships, 12.2s behind winner Vladimir Kuts, but a fortnight later turned the tables at a London v. Moscow athletics competition, setting a world record time of 13m:51.6s. The contest was televised via the Eurovision network and made Chataway a sporting celebrity. Chataway retired from international athletics after competing at the 1956 Olympic Games.

Five Nations Rugby

Position	Nation	Played	Won	Draw	Lost	For	Against	+/-	Points
1st	**Wales**	4	3	0	1	52	34	+18	6
1st	**England**	4	3	0	1	39	23	+16	6
1st	**France**	4	3	0	1	35	22	+13	6
4th	Ireland	4	1	0	3	18	34	-16	2
5th	Scotland	4	0	0	4	6	37	-31	0

The 1954 and twenty-fifth series of the rugby union Five Nations Championship saw ten matches played between the 9th January and the 10th April. Including the previous incarnations as the Home Nations and Five Nations, this was the sixtieth series of the northern hemisphere rugby union championship. Contested by England, France, Ireland, Scotland and Wales, the championship was shared by Wales, England and France.

Date	Team	Score	Team	Location
09-01-1954	Scotland	0-3	France	Edinburgh
16-01-1954	England	9-6	Wales	London
23-01-1954	France	8-0	Ireland	Paris
13-02-1954	England	14-3	Ireland	London
27-02-1954	Ireland	6-0	Scotland	Belfast
13-03-1954	Ireland	9-12	Wales	Dublin
20-03-1954	Scotland	3-13	England	Edinburgh
27-03-1954	Wales	19-13	France	Cardiff
10-04-1954	France	11-3	England	Paris
10-04-1954	Wales	15-3	Scotland	Swansea

Nation	Venue(s)	Captain(s)
England	Twickenham	Bob Stirling
France	Stade Olympique Yves-du-Manoir	Jean Prat
Ireland	Lansdowne Road / Ravenhill	Jackie Kyle / Jim McCarthy
Scotland	Murrayfield	Norman Davidson / Doug Elliot
Wales	National Stadium / St Helen's	Ken Jones / Rees Stephens / Rex Willis

Calcutta Cup

Scotland 3-13 England

The Calcutta Cup was first awarded in 1879 and is the rugby union trophy awarded to the winner of the match (currently played as part of the Six Nations Championship) between England and Scotland. The Cup was presented to the Rugby Football Union after the Calcutta Football Club in India disbanded in 1878; it is made from melted down silver rupees withdrawn from the club's funds.

Historical Standings (2023)	England	Scotland	Draws
	71 Wins	43 Wins	16

BRITISH GRAND PRIX

1954 British Grand Prix winner José Froilán González.

The 1954 British Grand Prix was held at Silverstone on the 17th July and was race 5 of 9 in the World Championship of Drivers. The race was won by Ferrari driver José Froilán González over 90 laps of the 2.927-mile circuit.

Pos.	Driver	Country	Car
1	**José Froilán González**	**Argentina**	**Ferrari**
2	Mike Hawthorn	United Kingdom	Ferrari
3	Onofre Marimón	Argentina	Maserati

Fun facts: The Silverstone circuit is built on the site of the World War II Royal Air Force bomber station, RAF Silverstone, and first hosted the British Grand Prix in 1948.

1954 GRAND PRIX SEASON

	Date	Race	Circuit	Winning Driver	Constructor
1.	17-01	Argentine GP	Autódromo	Juan Manuel Fangio	Maserati
2.	31-05	Indianapolis 500	Indianapolis	Bill Vukovich	Kurtis-Offenhauser
3.	20-06	Belgian GP	Spa	Juan Manuel Fangio	Maserati
4.	04-07	French GP	Reims-Gueux	Juan Manuel Fangio	Mercedes
5.	17-07	British GP	Silverstone	José Froilán González	Ferrari
6.	01-08	German GP	Nürburgring	Juan Manuel Fangio	Mercedes
7.	22-08	Swiss GP	Bremgarten	Juan Manuel Fangio	Mercedes
8.	05-09	Italian GP	Monza	Juan Manuel Fangio	Mercedes
9.	23-10	Spanish GP	Pedralbes	Mike Hawthorn	Ferrari

The 1954 Grand Prix season was won by Juan Manuel Fangio of Argentina who drove and won races for both Maserati and Mercedes-Benz throughout the series (making him the only driver in F1 history to win a championship driving for more than one team in the same season). José Froilán González finished the season in second place and Britain's Mike Hawthorn finished in third.

GRAND NATIONAL - ROYAL TAN

Royal Tan being led in after winning the 1954 Grand National at Aintree.

The 1954 Grand National was the 108th renewal of this world famous horse race and took place at Aintree Racecourse near Liverpool on the 27th March. The race was won by ten-year-old gelding Royal Tan, trained by Vincent O'Brien and ridden by Bryan Marshall.

Of the 29 runners only 9 horses actually completed the course; of the others: 15 fell, 3 refused, 1 pulled up and another unseated its rider. *NB: The race resulted in four equine fatalities.*

EPSOM DERBY - NEVER SAY DIE

The Derby Stakes is Britain's richest horse race and the most prestigious of the country's five Classics. First run in 1780 this Group 1 flat horse race is open to 3-year-old thoroughbred colts and fillies. The race takes place at Epsom Downs in Surrey over a distance of one mile, four furlongs and 10 yards (2,423 metres) and is scheduled for early June each year. The 1954 Derby was won by Never Say Die, ridden by jockey Lester Piggott. *Photo: American-bred, British-trained racehorse Never Say Die (1951-1975) after winning the 1954 Epsom Derby.*

Football League Champions

England

Pos.	Team	W	D	L	F	A	Pts.
1	**Wolverhampton Wanderers**	**25**	**7**	**10**	**96**	**56**	**57**
2	West Bromwich Albion	22	9	11	86	63	53
3	Huddersfield Town	20	11	11	78	61	51
4	Manchester United	18	12	12	73	58	48
5	Bolton Wanderers	18	12	12	75	60	48

Scotland

Pos.	Team	W	D	L	F	A	Pts.
1	**Celtic**	**20**	**3**	**7**	**72**	**29**	**43**
2	Heart of Midlothian	16	6	8	70	45	38
3	Partick Thistle	17	1	12	76	54	35
4	Rangers	13	8	9	56	35	34
5	Hibernian	15	4	11	72	51	34

FA Cup - West Bromwich Albion

West Bromwich Albion   3-2   Preston North End

The 1954 FA Cup Final took place on the 1st May at Wembley Stadium in front of 100,000 fans. The game saw West Bromwich Albion beat Preston North End 3-2 to lift the Cup for the fourth time. *Photo: West Bromwich Albion captain, Len Millard, holds the FA Cup aloft while his team mates carry him around Wembley Stadium after their 1954 FA Cup triumph.*

SNOOKER - FRED DAVIS

Fred Davis 45-26 Walter Donaldson

The 1954 World Professional Match-play Championship was held across several venues around the U.K. between the 5th October 1953 and the 6th March 1954. The final was contested by Fred Davis and Walter Donaldson, with Davis defeating Donaldson 45-26 in the 71-frame final. The highest break of the tournament (121) was made by Donaldson on the last day of the final. *Photo: Fred Davis (left) and Walter Donaldson c.1948.*

GOLF - OPEN CHAMPIONSHIP - PETER THOMSON

The 1954 Open Championship was the 83rd to be played and was held between the 7th and 9th July at Royal Birkdale Golf Club in Southport, England. Peter Thomson of Australia won the first of his five Open titles by one stroke over runners-up Bobby Locke, Dai Rees and Syd Scott. *NB: This was the first time the championship had been held at Royal Birkdale. Photo: Peter Thomson, aged 23, receives the Claret Jug from S.T.L. Greer (the Captain of the Royal Birkdale Golf Club) after his British Open Championship win.*

WIMBLEDON

Men's Singles Champion - Jaroslav Drobný - Egypt
Ladies Singles Champion - Maureen Connolly - United States

The 1954 Wimbledon Championships took place on the outdoor grass courts at the All England Lawn Tennis and Croquet Club in Wimbledon, London. It ran from the 21st June until the 3rd July and was the third Grand Slam tennis event of 1954.

Men's Singles Final

Country	Player	Set 1	Set 2	Set 3	Set 4
Egypt	Jaroslav Drobný	13	4	6	9
Australia	Ken Rosewall	11	6	2	7

Women's Singles Final

Country	Player	Set 1	Set 2
United States	Maureen Connolly	6	7
United States	Louise Brough	2	5

Men's Doubles Final

Country	Players	Set 1	Set 2	Set 3	Set 4
Australia	Rex Hartwig / Mervyn Rose	6	6	3	6
United States	Vic Seixas / Tony Trabert	4	4	6	4

Women's Doubles Final

Country	Players	Set 1	Set 2	Set 3
United States	Louise Brough / Margaret duPont	4	9	6
United States	Shirley Fry / Doris Hart	6	7	3

Mixed Doubles Final

Country	Players	Set 1	Set 2	Set 3
United States	Vic Seixas / Doris Hart	5	6	6
Australia / United States	Ken Rosewall / Margaret duPont	7	4	3

County Championship Cricket - Surrey

1954 saw the fifty-fifth officially organised running of the County Championship. It ran from the 8th May until the 1st September, and was Surrey's third of seven successive County Championships wins.

Pos.	Team	Pld.	W	L	D	Tie	Pts.
1	**Surrey**	**28**	**15**	**3**	**8**	**0**	**208**
2	Yorkshire	28	13	3	8	1	186
3	Derbyshire	28	11	6	9	0	168

Test Matches

England 1-1 Pakistan

Game	Ground	Result
1	Lord's, London	Match drawn
2	Trent Bridge, Nottingham	England won by an innings and 129 runs
3	Old Trafford, Manchester	Match drawn
4	The Oval, London	Pakistan won by 24 runs

1954 British Empire & Commonwealth Games

The 1954 British Empire & Commonwealth Games were held in held in Vancouver, Canada, from the 30th July until the 7th August. The games were attended by 24 nations and 662 competitors.

Medals Table:

Rank	Nation	Gold	Silver	Bronze	Total
1	**England**	23	24	20	67
2	Australia	20	11	17	48
3	South Africa	16	6	13	35
4	Canada	9	20	14	43
5	New Zealand	7	7	5	19
6	Scotland	6	2	5	13
9	Northern Ireland	2	1	0	3
13	Wales	1	1	5	7

THE COST OF LIVING

Blow me! They're wonderful!

Life's always sweeter with Spangles

All Fruit flavour Spangles contain natural fruit extracts and other fine flavours.

only 3ᵈ a packet

COMPARISON CHART

	1954	1954 (+ Inflation)	2023	% Change
3 Bedroom House	£2,950	£97,936	£281,272	+187.2%
Weekly Income	£6.4s.10d	£207.21	£640	+208.9%
Pint Of Beer	11d	£1.52	£4.19	+175.7%
Cheese (lb)	2s.7d	£4.29	£3.23	-24.7%
Bacon (lb)	2s.9d	£4.56	£3.79	-16.9%
The Beano	2d	28p	£2.99	+967.9%

GROCERIES - SHOPPING

Bread Loaf	7½d
Eggs (dozen)	4s
Butter (½lb)	1s.10½d
Milk (pint)	7d
St Ivel Cheese	10½d
Cow & Gate Cheese Spread	1s.1d
Sugar (per lb)	7½d
Quaker Oats	9½d
Carsons Mascot Chocolates & Candies (¼ lb)	1s
Mackintosh's Toff-o-Luxe Toffee (pkt.)	4½d
Fry's Milk Punch Bar	4d
Potatoes (per lb)	2d
Apples (per lb)	11¼d
Oranges (per lb)	1s
Bisto Gravy (4oz carton)	7½d
Lyons Orange Maid Ice Lolly	6d
Silvikrin Shampoo (liquid)	6d
Vaseline Soapless Shampoo (pkt.)	4½d
Ever Ready Razor Set	11s.6d
DenClen Denture Cleaner (3 months' supply)	2s.7½d
Cosmedin Beauty Lotion	4s.6d
Cutex Nail Polish	2s.3d
Aspro (pkt.)	1s.8d
Rexall Plenamins Vitamin Capsules (15 days)	5s
Rinso Washing Powder (giant size)	1s.6d
Zal Pine Disinfectant (big value bottle)	1s
Booth's Dry Gin (bottle)	£1.13s.9d
Dry Fly Sherry (half bottle)	10s.6d
Whiteway's Pomona Vintage Cyder (bottle)	5s
The Three Castles Cigarettes (20)	3s.11d
Woman's Weekly Magazine	4½d
Daily Mirror Newspaper	1½d

Haliborange

KEEPS THE FAMILY FLOURISHING

In bottles 3/6 from Chemists only

The nicest way of taking Halibut Oil

MADE BY ALLEN & HANBURYS LTD.

More and more people...

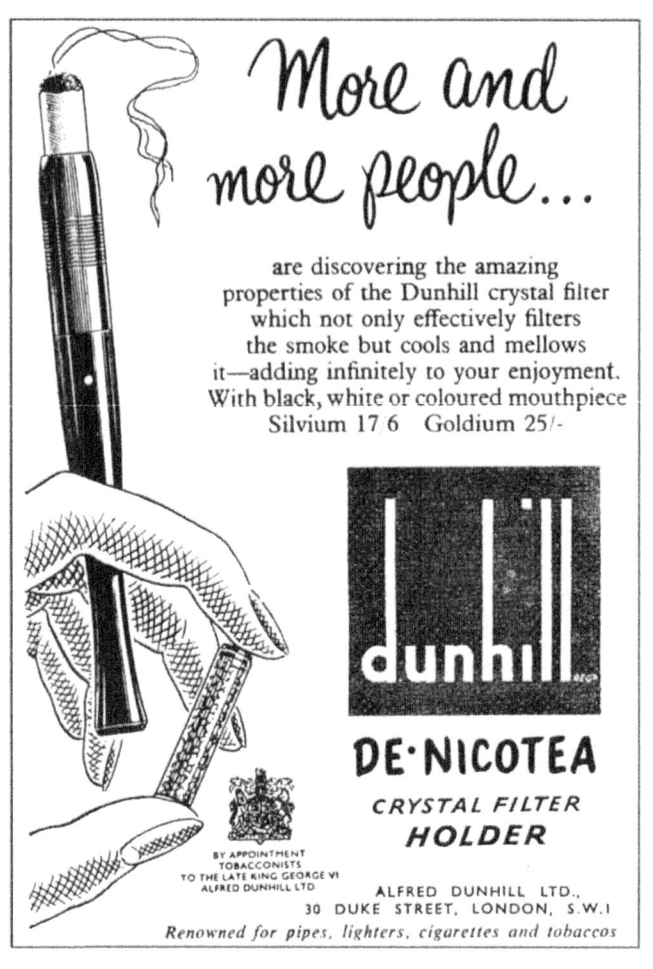

are discovering the amazing properties of the Dunhill crystal filter which not only effectively filters the smoke but cools and mellows it—adding infinitely to your enjoyment. With black, white or coloured mouthpiece
Silvium 17/6   Goldium 25/-

dunhill
DE·NICOTEA
CRYSTAL FILTER **HOLDER**

BY APPOINTMENT
TOBACCONISTS
TO THE LATE KING GEORGE VI
ALFRED DUNHILL LTD

ALFRED DUNHILL LTD.,
30 DUKE STREET, LONDON, S.W.1
Renowned for pipes, lighters, cigarettes and tobaccos

GROOMED

for the occasion —with Straight 8 of course

Brilliantine
3 oz. 1/10
4 oz. 2/3

STRAIGHT 8

AFTER-SHAVE LOTION, SHAVING CREAM, BRILLIANTINE, OIL OF ROSES

CLOTHES

Women's Clothing

Leslie Marshall Tulip Line Coat	£8.19s.6d
Darrell Mills Tailored Raincoat	£7.15s
Fashion Values Mac	£1.6s.6d
Helena Smith Princess Line Corduroy Suit	£5.19s.6d
Mansell Zip Fronted Housecoat	£2.2ss
D. Conway & Co. Corduroy Dress	£1.10s
Jove Household Products Pinarettes (x2)	3s.11d
A.Z. Skirt Co. Blended Wool Maternity Skirt	18s.6d
Supreme Fashion Outsize Skirt	17s.6d
Rossmere 80% Wool Dressing Gown	17s.6d
Briar Rose Rayon Nightdress	£3.3s
Gossard Nylon Plunge Bra	15s.3d
Ambrose Wilson Corset	15s.11d
Gossard Elastic Girdle	£2.2s
Dunlop Seamless Wellingtons	15s.9d
Duraflex Bootees	£3.9s.9d
Duraflex Cushion Tread Shoes	£2.15s.9d
G.L. Brown Slippers / House Shoes	12s.6d

Men's Clothing

Govt. Surplus Melton Greatcoat	£2.15s
Royal Navy Black Oilskin Coat	£1.9s.11d
Majestic Reconditioned Police Raincoat	£1.15s.11d
Maenson Double Breasted Suit	18gns
Chatham Drill Shirts (x3)	£1.3s
Canadian Pure Wool Khaki Shirt	12s.6d
H.J. Boulting Plastic Permanent Knot Tie (x3)	10s.6d
Metropolitan Police Serge Trousers	18s.9d
J.M. Trading Co. Army Boots	15s.6d
Ashers RAF & Naval Oxford Style Shoes	£1.4s.11d
J.M. Trading House Slippers	12s.6d

Don't let your trousers let you down!

'UNDER' CONTROL BY **Sphere BRACES**

SPHERE SUSPENDERS, BRACES, BELTS AND GARTERS STAND PRE-EMINENT

FAIRE BROS & CO., LTD., RUTLAND STREET, LEICESTER

Hand tailored fine wool check tweed suit for country wear. Single breasted three-buttoned jacket. Side wrap at back and front of skirt. Suit illustrated chosen from our stock range. In sizes 12, 14, 16 and 18. Price £22. 15. 0.

MOSS BROS
& CO LTD
OF COVENT GARDEN

Junction of Garrick and Bedford Streets, W.C.2

*TEMPLE BAR 4477
and Branches*

JOYCET Regd.
Gives Girdle Confidence

— like having a second skin, this wonderful JOYCET girdle — **stays in place, however active you are.** JOYCET girdles — there is a choice of FOUR — are lightweight garments designed with skilfully cut sections, finely tailored to Fashion's newest line, while giving the necessary support. The JOYCET came into being through the TWILFIT designer's careful study of BODY MOVEMENT — each of the cleverly cut sections of which it is composed is so placed to take the natural pull of the body **AND TO RESIST "RIDING UP"** — with its **even weight** throughout, the JOYCET is cool and comfortable in all temperatures.

Prices from 35/11 to 55/-
AT ALL GOOD SHOPS

JOYCET—**will not** ride up!

Write for the Illustrated Booklet to

(DEPT. A3) LEETHEMS (TWILFIT) LTD. PORTSMOUTH

A *Twilfit* CREATION

OTHER PRICES

Vauxhall Cresta Car (inc. tax)	£844.0s.10d
Aquatex Car Cover	£1.7s.3d
BSA 500cc B33 Motorcycle (inc. tax)	£168.12s
Batley Concrete Garage	£46
Watford Cycle's Rebuilt Light Roadster Bicycles	£7.10s
Casablanca First Class Return Flight	£76
Milan Return Flight	£34.4s
Geneva Return Flight	£18.4s
Austria Independent Inclusive Holiday (16 days)	£23.10s
London Service Apartment (per day)	from £1.15s
Andrew Page Speaking Doll	£2.19s.6d
Kids Wigwam Tent	£1.5s
Waddington's Monopoly Game	19s.11d
Waddington's Cluedo Game	19s.11d
Dinky Toy Jaguar XK120 Coupe	2s.8d
RGD 17in Console B&W TV (inc. tax)	110gns
Piccolo Cine Projector	£4.19s.6d
Alan Richards A.C. Electric Paint Sprayer	£3.15s
Eatons Big-Top Paraffin Heater	£1.3s.6d
Remington 60 Electric Shaver	£9.17s.11d
Res-Rite 6ft 2in x 4ft 8in Divan Bed	£3.10s
Triune Co. Blended Woollen Blanket	15s.11d
Direct Supply Co. Flannelette Sheet	9s.11d
J.A. Davis 17-Jewel Swiss Pin Lever Watch	£8.7s.6d
Timex Algold Wrist Watch	£4.2s
Pigskin Lightweight Cigarette Case (holds 20)	£8.10s
Royal Worcester Teapot	£1.18s.9d
Church's Alabastine Crack Filler	1s.3d

The resorts in the BERNESE OBERLAND

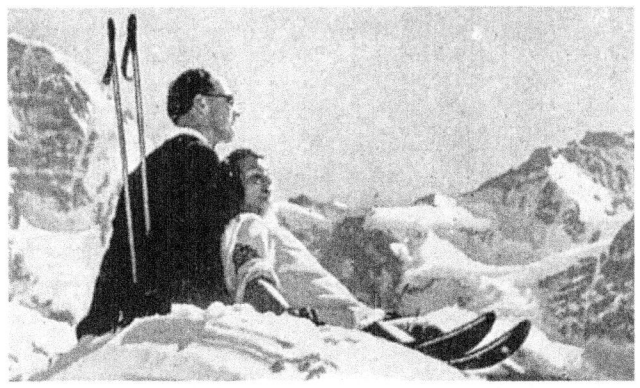

(150 Hotels with over 7,000 beds. 25 Lifts. Ski and Skating Schools)

• Winter Season from Christmas to Easter

• reduced rates in January

Average 10 days all inclusive rates in very good Hotels
£14·0·0 (room, 3 meals, tips, taxes, etc. included)

Prospectus and Information: VBO-Office Interlaken, Switzerland, the Swiss National Tourist Office: 458/9 Strand, London, W.C.2, or your Travel Agent.

IVA ZURICH

MONEY CONVERSION TABLE

Pounds / Shillings / Pence 1954 'Old Money'	Decimal Value	Value 2023 (Rounded)
Farthing	¼d	0.1p	3p
Half Penny	½d	0.21p	7p
Penny	1d	0.42p	14p
Threepence	3d	1.25p	41p
Sixpence	6d	2.5p	83p
Shilling	1s	5p	£1.66
Florin	2s	10p	£3.32
Half Crown	2s.6d	12.5p	£4.15
Crown	5s	25p	£8.30
Ten Shillings	10s	50p	£16.60
Pound	20s	£1	£32.20
Guinea	21s	£1.05	£34.86
Five Pounds	£5	£5	£165.99
Ten Pounds	£10	£10	£331.99

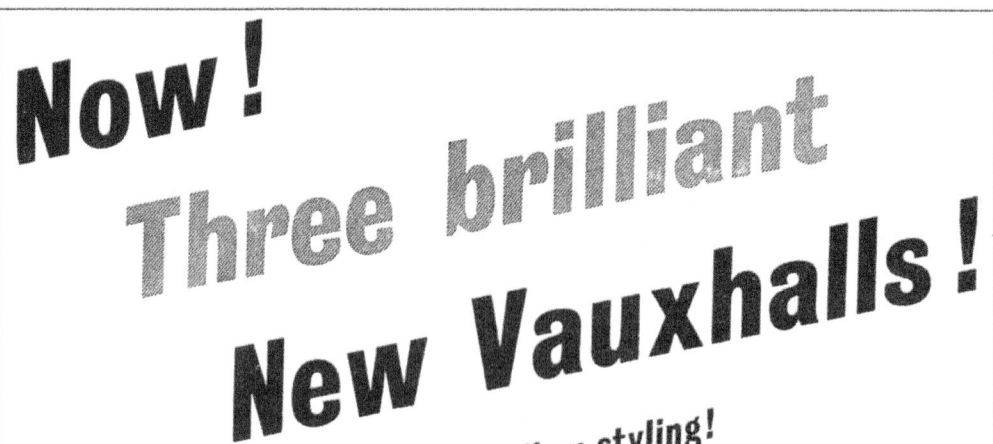

Now! Three brilliant New Vauxhalls!

New styling!
New colour schemes!
New de-luxe interiors!
New Value!

The Sparkling New Cresta

Spacious . . . Powerful . . . Economical . . . That's Vauxhall value!

Gordon's

Stands Supreme

MAXIMUM PRICES: BOT. 33/9d · ½ BOT. 17/7d · ¼ BOT. 9/2d · MINIATURE 3/7d · U.K. ONLY

Printed in Great Britain
by Amazon